An Unauthorized Biography of

Charles Krauthammer

The Renowned Journalist, Political Pundit, and Pulitzer Prize Winner

By Malcolm Stone

All rights reserved © 2017 Malcolm Stone

Cover image licensed under Creative Commons Attribution 2.0 Generic license (https://creativecommons.org/licenses/by-sa/2.0/). Author of image is www.GlynLowe.com (https://www.flickr.com/photos/glynlowe/). The author of the image has not endorsed this work. Image hosted at Flickr.

Table of Contents

1. Introduction
2. Family
3. Early Life
4. Early Political Thought
5. Developing New Interests
6. The Accident
7. Marriage and Medical Career
8. Early Years at the New Republic
9. The Reagan Doctrine
10. Journalistic Prestige
11. The Unipolar Moment
12. Television
13. Return to McGill
14. Conservative Journalist
15. Fox News
16. The Aftermath of 9/11
17. The George W. Bush Administration
18. Marcel's Passing
19. Presidential Election of 2008
20. Bestselling Author
21. Presidential Election of 2016
22. Conclusions

1. Introduction

Charles Krauthammer is an American author, political pundit, and columnist who has been a fixture in the American political scene since the 1980s. Krauthammer has a weekly newspaper column that reaches more than 400 newspapers through global syndication. He makes frequent appearances on the Fox News network, including *Special Report with Bret Baier*, where he is a regular panelist.

Krauthammer has also endured hardship and excellent in multiple pursuits. After a serious accident that left him partially paralyzed, he married and became a doctor. He then moved to Washington, D.C. and became involved in politics. Krauthammer has been married to his wife, Robyn, since 1974, and the couple has a son named Daniel. His story is one of intellectual brilliance and tenacity.

His prominence as a journalist is due largely to his approach to intellectualism. He is not a zealot. He actively avoids being caught up in manias and fads. He also refuses to reveal too much about himself, eschewing subjectivity and focusing instead on universal, generalizable truths. At heart, he is a conservative, seeking to maintain what is good about modern society. His clear thinking and breadth of knowledge, however, distinguish him from other conservative thinkers.

2. Family

Born on March 13, 1950 to Thea Krauthammer in New York, young Charles Krauthammer was influenced heavily by his father, Shulim Krauthammer. Reflecting on his childhood, he observes that, his father "had a life, 1903-1987, that basically is the story of the 20th Century…" Born in the Ukraine, the senior Krauthammer moved to Lyons, France at sixteen. He made his living as a mushroom distributor. Eventually, though, he fought in Italy in World War II, as part of the French tank corps. Charles Krauthammer remembers his father always carrying with him the double cross, which was the symbol of the French resistance.

The senior Krauthammer then emigrated to Cuba, where he spent the remaining war years manufacturing materials for the U.S. army and hiring European refugees. In Cuba, he met his future wife and married her. The pair traveled to post-war Europe, and then emigrated to the United States. There, they started a family.

Charles Krauthammer was five years old when his family moved to Montreal, Quebec. The move was due to his father's work, but his father also liked the idea of living where people frequently spoke French. Shulim Krauthammer was a lawyer who entered the real estate business.

Canadian politician John Ciaccia remembers working with Shulim Krauthammer as a young attorney:

At the new firm, I met colourful characters who had equally colourful stories to tell…. There was Shulim Krauthammer, who used to regale me with fascinating stories of Leon Blum, the first Jewish president of France (and who he claimed had been his friend) who resisted the Vichy regime, was imprisoned by the Nazis, and miraculously survived. Shulim was having problems with one of the firm's clients, Peter Issenman, regarding land that Shulim had sold him in St Bruno, a short distance from downtown Montreal. "Johnny," he told me in his thick accent one day, "if I had an atom bomb, I would drop it on St Bruno." "Mr. Krauthammer," I replied, "if you dropped an atom bomb on St Bruno, it would also destroy this office building where I'm working." "Don't worry," he reassured me. "If I had the power to have an atom bomb, I would also have the power it shouldn't affect you in Place Ville Marie."

Something of the senior Krauthammer's wit and enthusiasm rubbed off on young Charles Krauthammer. Charles also benefited from his father's industriousness. Despite being a recent immigrant, Shulim Krauthammer provided well for his family, and they never had to worry about financial distress.

3. Early Life

In Montreal, Krauthammer was enrolled in Jewish day school. There were two school systems in Montreal, one Protestant and the other Catholic. With unintentional humor, the sign outside of his school read, "United Talmud Torahs of Montreal, Protestant School Board," because every non-Catholic school fell under the purview of the Protestant School Board. Despite that fact, the education was true to Judaism. This focus instilled a deep sense of appreciation for both Judaism and Jewish culture in Krauthammer. He recalls that:

My father thought I didn't get enough Talmud at school, so I took the extra Talmud class at school and he had a rabbi come to the house three nights a week. One of those nights was Saturday night, so in synagogue Saturday morning my brother and I would pray very hard for snow so he wouldn't be able to come on Saturday night and we could watch hockey night in Canada. That's where I learned about prayer.

The family, consisting of Charles, his older (by four years) brother Marcel, and his parents, spent their summers at a vacation home in Long Beach, New York. Krauthammer remembers time spent playing on the beach, and home movies of his early childhood vacations exist. While Krauthammer is proud of his Canadian upbringing, he was also an American from birth and throughout his childhood. From age five, his was truly a dual citizenship.

At home, Krauthammer's parents refused to buy a television, preferring to enjoy time together as a family instead. Although he has frequently mentioned the absence of television, Charles has never complained about it, except in the case of the weekly hockey game broadcast. He was an intelligent and resourceful child, and had no trouble filling his time with productive activities. Krauthammer recalls having a pet turtle, which died after it became lodged behind a radiator. His brother had a parakeet, which eventually escaped through a window.

During Krauthammer's formative years in the 1950's and '60's, Quebec was caught up in what he calls an "anti-colonial struggle," as the French citizens struggled to overcome the rule of Quebec's Anglo minority. The movement sometimes involved violence, including terrorism. Krauthammer and his brother were told not to go near mailboxes for fear of bombs, and a bomb did, in fact, go off in a mailbox near his home.

He explains that, "I was considered Anglo, even though my family's French-speaking... We spoke French at home, but because we're Jewish we were considered Anglos."

In addition to social issues, science and religion were on the mind of the young Krauthammer. He attended the 1964-65 New York World's Fair as a teenager. He recalls visiting a display called "Sermons from Science." The attraction featured films about scientific principles that grabbed his intention. The miracles of science, however, were followed by a sermon about how scientific wonders demonstrated the existence of God. Krauthammer knew he had been tricked. The whole presentation had come courtesy of the Moody

Bible Institute. "That was my first unhappy encounter with the use of science for nonscientific ends."

4. Early Political Thought

At age 16, Krauthammer graduated from high school (in a class of 28 students), and began attending McGill University in Montreal, where he eventually earned an undergraduate degree in political science and economics, while experiencing firsthand the political upheavals of that period.

Unlike the United States, where Vietnam War protests attracted college students in the 1960's, Quebec experienced ant-British colonialism protests.

In 1968, McGill experienced a 10-day student occupation of the Political Science and Economics department. This led to an administrative review of the unrest, as well as disagreement among university officials. One political science professor, Stanley Gray, was fired as a result. The radical Gray, a Marxist, led a protest on campus in March 1969, which involved several thousand protesters.

Krauthammer recalls witnessing a demonstration when he was a junior, at about age 18, that involved both communists and fascists, including Stanley Gray. This was almost surely the March 1969 demonstration. The young Krauthammer was not persuaded by either extremist camp involved. Instead, he expresses gratitude that the event, "cleansed me very early in my political evolution of any romanticism. I detested the extreme left and the extreme right, and found myself somewhere in the middle." He came to realize, as many others noted, that the extreme left and the extreme right frequently converge, as they did in 1930's Germany.

In 1969, Krauthammer was elected to be editor of McGill's student newspaper, The Daily. The September 25, 1969 issue of the paper reports that Krauthammer was the Arts and Science representative of the Student Council at the time of his election; he beat out five competitors, winning the final vote by ten to two.

As editor, Krauthammer replaced the newspaper's Maoist slant with a focus on pluralism, announcing to readers that the paper would consider all views, instead of promoting a particular ideology.

Harold Waller, a professor of political science at McGill, notes that, "The Daily then, and probably now, was very biased in one direction. With the exception of 1970, when Charlie Krauthammer [now a neoconservative columnist for the Washington Post and Fox News contributor] was the editor, then it was a very sensible newspaper."

The McGill Daily absorbed a huge portion of Krauthammer's time. He recalls one incident in which he stayed up all night rewriting editorials, remaining alert by drinking copious amounts of coffee. By morning, he was so sick of coffee that he swore it off permanently.

One influential professor during Krauthammer's time at McGill was Rabbi David Hartman, who taught a course on the Jewish philosopher, Maimonides. The combination of Judaism and Aristotelian philosophy was intriguing to Krauthammer, who says the course reinforced his identification with Judaism at a time when he was becoming less religious.

5. Developing New Interests

Krauthammer graduated from college at the top of his class at age 20. He spent some time as a Commonwealth Scholar of politics at Balliol College, one of the constituent colleges of the University of Oxford in 1970 and 1971. He also received a Woodrow Wilson Fellowship in 1970. At Oxford, he became interested in the political writings of John Stuart Mill, who would remain a strong influence on his thinking. However, Krauthammer ultimately ended up changing his academic focus when he decided to attend Harvard's Medical School.

One other important event happened at Oxford, though. Krauthammer met Robyn Trethewey, an Australian law student who would soon become his wife. She would first travel to Paris to work as an attorney, but would later travel to the United States to pursue marriage and art. While the pair were apart, they wrote letters to each other.

On a trip to Cambridge, Massachusetts at age 20, Krauthammer discovered one of his lifelong loves. He saw a friend's roommate sitting with a chess clock and asked about the game. He ended up playing from 10:00 pm to 5:00 am the next day. "I had found something that I loved, and I was in deep trouble."

Over the ensuing years, Krauthammer would repeatedly discuss chess in his articles. For the ambitious, goal-driven man, chess seems to be something of a guilty pleasure. In a 1983 article titled "The Romance of Chess," Krauthammer defended the game against charges that it was a frivolous waste of time. He seemed to be convincing himself as well as the reader. He acknowledged that, "I don't intend a total defense of chess. I have spent—wasted—too many hours at the board for that."

In a tongue-in-cheek 1995 article, "Cyberaddict, Share My Cure," he admitted that the game was "an entirely useless, self-referential experience," although "totally absorbing." He then explained that his technique for overcoming his chess addiction was to use the psychological cure of flooding. He would play for a long stretch, until "my mind is numb and my eyes are crossed," playing to the point where the game became repulsive. He would then be free of its attractions for a while.

Years later, he would join the "Pariah Chess Club" with conservatives Dinesh D'Souza and Charles Murray. For the college-age Krauthammer, however, those future developments would have been unimaginable.

6. The Accident

During his first year in medical school, in 1972, Krauthammer had an accident that would significantly alter his life. On a summer day, Krauthammer and a friend were swimming in the Children's Inn's outdoor swimming pool, next door to Boston's Children's Hospital.

Diving off a diving board, Krauthammer accidentally hit his head on the cement. The impact severed part of his spine, and he was immobilized at the bottom of the pool.

"I knew exactly what had happened. And I knew I was going to die, because I couldn't swim. And at a certain point, when that happens, you don't panic anymore. And it was at that point that they pulled me out."

Krauthammer was left paralyzed from the waist down. He was hospitalized for over a year and experienced complications including pneumonia. After he was well enough to leave, he followed a strict exercise regimen for a couple of years, and was able to gain partial mobility in his hands and arms, which enabled him to write.

He prefers not to talk about his accident and the resulting paralysis, and does not agree with those who find his suffering heroic. "There's nothing ennobling about disease," he explains. "And there's nothing degrading about it. It's a condition of life." Later, when the AIDS epidemic hit America, he would apply the same reasoning to that issue, concluding that it was an error to apply moral judgment to a disease, which is just a condition of life.

The accident seems to have led Krauthammer to think deeply, however, about when life is worth living. The issue of whether life can be so bad that death is preferable has arisen several times in his writing over the years. In a 1985 article entitled, "What to Do About 'Baby Doe,'" Krauthammer concludes that there is a life so damaged that mercy favors ending it. He quotes Richard McCormick, a philosopher, for the proposition that, "Life is a relative good, and the duty to preserve it a limited one... Life is a value to be preserved only insofar as it contains some potentiality for human relationships."

Krauthammer's subsequent life has demonstrated that his accident came nowhere close to remove the potentiality for human relationships from his life. Implicit in his subsequent writings, however, is the fact that his injury made him think deeply about such issues.

Some commentators have speculated that the accident led to Krauthammer's rejection of religion in favor of agnosticism, but he insists that that is not the case. For intellectual reasons, he became non-religious in his late teens, while his accident did not occur until he was 22 years old. In fact, he notes that the question of "why me?" did not appeal to him after the accident. He quickly decided to get on with his life, even though he was of course very unhappy about the development.

If there is a positive side to the accident for Krauthammer, it is that he believes his accident has made him more sensitive to others who suffer.

Krauthammer did sue the company that had built the swimming pool where he was injured. He was not vindictive, but it was clear that he would bear some significant financial costs due to his injury, and he believed that the flawed design of the pool caused his injury. After five years, the parties settled out of court, and he received one million dollars. That money helped him pay for wheelchair-accessible vans and the like before he became financially successful.

For Krauthammer, though, the physical complications of his injury would continue for life. In 1982, for example, he acknowledged being absent for a four-day hospital stay relating to back pain. It was not, however, his only hospital visit of the year. Although he seldom acknowledges these issues publicly, Krauthammer has clearly endured many hospital visits over the years.

7. Marriage and Medical Career

Despite the injury, Krauthammer continued to pursue his ambitions. After the accident, he had worried about what his personal life would become. He stopped writing to Robyn, assuming, perhaps, that she would not want to marry someone with a severe medical disability. Robyn learned about the accident months later, and eventually traveled to visit him in fall of 1973. In 1974, the couple married. Robyn also converted to Judaism.

Krauthammer also continued his studies at Harvard. The university accommodated his disability, allowing him to take test orally, for example, and he earned his medical doctorate in 1975. At Harvard, he earned the DuPont-Warren Fellowship.

Following his graduation, Krauthammer went on to Massachusetts General Hospital, where he was initially a resident physician for the hospital's psychiatry department. He recalls that residents were required to participate in group-therapy meetings each week, but that he refused to attend. After a few weeks, the departing chair questioned him about his refusal to attend and was told that he must attend or be removed from the program. He attended grudgingly. "I said nary a word in the group. I was occasionally asked why. 'I'm in denial,' I explained."

Despite that one incident of civil disobedience, it seems that Krauthammer excelled in his residency. He received the Edwin Dunlop Prize for being the "Top Psychiatric Resident" in 1978. Today, he remembers his time as a resident fondly.

After being promoted to chief resident, Krauthammer published work outlining a new form of manic depression that he called "Secondary Mania," written with Professor Gerald Klerman. The American Board of Psychiatry and Neurology granted board certification to Krauthammer in 1984.

In 1978, Krauthammer left Massachusetts General Hospital to take a position with the National Institute of Mental Health. Klerman, the professor with whom he had coauthored papers, had received a presidential appointment to head up a new agency (the Alcohol, Drug Abuse, and Mental Health Administration), and he had persuaded Krauthammer to take the government post.

Krauthammer also met Martin Kaplan, a speechwriter for Vice President Walter Mondale during Carter's reelection campaign in 1980. Kaplan hired Krauthammer to write speeches with him. After six months at that post, however, Mondale's presidential aspirations ended.

Hendrik Hertzberg of *The New Yorker* recalls meeting Krauthammer in 1978, shortly after he left his medical practice. He recalls that Krauthammer's views at the time were "70 percent Mondale liberal, 30 percent 'Scoop Jackson Democrat,' i.e., hard-line on Israel and relations with the Soviet Union."

Krauthammer had become interested in writing about politics, so he applied for a position at *The New Republic*. Michael Kinsley of *The New Republic* recalls that, "I got his 'resume' and it said he was a psychiatrist and I thought, 'God this is bizarre.'" Kinsley gave him a chance, though, and

Krauthammer accepted a position as a writer and editor on January 20, 1981, just as Ronald Reagan's first term as President began. Krauthammer would continue being a regular contributor to *The New Republic* through 2011.

Although he had left the practice of medicine, he could not fully escape it. When he began his work at *The New Republic*, his co-workers learned of his medical credentials. He was forced to keep some medical supplies in his office, because writers who felt under the weather made a habit of coming to him for medical advice.

Krauthammer's early articles often focused on medical and psychiatric issues, as well. For example, his September 22, 1979 article, "The Expanding Shrink," addressed psychohistory, with Krauthammer admonishing readers to "Put psychiatry back in its place," and his December 22, 1979 article, "The Myth of Thomas Szasz" focused on the attempts of Szasz, the author of *The Myth of Mental Illness*, to undermine the diagnosis of mental illness.

Perhaps Krauthammer felt a need to prove that his psychiatric background could be useful to *The New Republic*, or perhaps it was natural for an expert in psychiatry to view contemporary issues from a psychiatric viewpoint. Whatever the reason, this early medical focus set the course for Krauthammer's subsequent writings, which have often touched on medical issues.

He was also unavoidably influenced by his own cultural roots. Commenting on Krauthammer's writing style, *New Republic* editor Martin Peretz noted that, "He has a very Jewish view of history. Many Jews have lived through in their historical consciousness the promises of the new tomorrow and the morrow turned out to be quite cruel."

Over the course of his career, Krauthammer would often display this type of historical consciousness, ever wary that the future has the potential for negative outcomes as well as positive ones. He would also occasionally discuss the plight of the world's Jews directly.

8. Early Years at the New Republic

From 1979 to 1983, Krauthammer wrote exclusively for the *New Republic*. One major theme of his early articles was experimentation on humans, and especially on human embryos. In "The Ethics of Human Experimentation," he examined the history of medical experimentation and asked when it is ethical to experiment on a consenting patient. In an article titled "Tales from the Hatchery," Krauthammer wondered how the public and courts would respond to medical technology enabling a baby to be developed in an artificial womb.

On a related theme, Krauthammer wrote about abortion. A June 6, 1981 article, "Science ex machina," found Krauthammer pointing out scientific flaws in the arguments of Senator John East, who sought to ban abortion.

A second emphasis in Krauthammer's early writings was the effect of oil importation on international politics. After the recent OPEC crisis, which left America and other Western countries with heavy debts, Krauthammer asked why an ODEC (Organization of Debt Exporting Countries) could not make demands just as the OPEC cartel does, in a piece titled "From OPEC to ODEC." In another article, he saw the cost of oil importation as a major factor in the economic plight of poor developing countries.

A third emphasis in Krauthammer's writings at this time was on nuclear armament. He would later describe this period as a time of mass hysteria about the threat of nuclear weapons, and this dominant Cold War theme found its way into many of his articles. In "How to Prevent a Nuclear War," he argued that any attempt to reduce America's nuclear arsenal should be combined with an increase in the country's conventional arsenal, and accused advocates of a nuclear freeze of undermining deterrence. In a subsequent article, "Half a Freeze," he praised nuclear freeze advocates for their efforts to reduce the world's arsenal of nuclear weapons, but again chided them for proceeding in a manner that would unilaterally weaken America.

At this early point in Krauthammer's career, it was already clear that he was at his most conservative when discussing international politics. While he might not have been a true realist, his writing was infused with the knowledge that the international world is chaotic and that the balance of power between countries is critically important.

On domestic issues, Krauthammer justifiably considered himself a liberal. In 1982, for example, he wrote a critique of the Supreme Court in which he accused Chief Justice Rehnquist of elevating personal property above individual liberty. In another article, comparing George Will and Michael Novak, he wrote that, "conservatives do indeed have ideas, but… on the whole they are contradictory."

9. The Reagan Doctrine

In 1983 Krauthammer began having essays published by *Time* magazine on a monthly basis, while continuing to write monthly pieces for the *New Republic*. Only four years into his writing career, he was one of the nation's premier columnists.

Over the course of the next two years (i.e., 1984 and 1985), Krauthammer continued to write about his favorite issues, but also devoted significant effort to issues of church and state. In 1984's "Perils of the Prophet Motive," he critiqued a letter from America's Catholic bishop on the topic of capitalism; while the bishops warned of the evils of capitalism and urged the nation to pursue more compassion policies, Krauthammer argued that the experience of nations shows that capitalism is the best policy for helping the poor. He noted that the bishops' letter "is no great contribution to political discourse." In "The Church-State Debate," Krauthammer addressed another political pronouncement from a religious leader, this one from the archbishop of New York, and argued that religious believers need not support laws imposing their beliefs on others.

Krauthammer's most notable writing continued to be in the area of international relations. Perhaps his most famous essay in *Time* described the Reagan Doctrine. U.S. Presidents had a tradition of announcing "doctrines" for foreign policy, delineating the approach they would take to international affairs. After President Reagan's 1985 State of the Union speech, Krauthammer famously identified a particular statement as the "Reagan Doctrine." The statement by Reagan was that:

We must not break faith with those who are risking their lives on every continent from Afghanistan to Nicaragua to defy Soviet-supported aggression and secure rights which have been ours from birth . . . Support for freedom fighters is self-defense.

Krauthammer interpreted this statement as a subtle disclosure of a major policy. According to Krauthammer's April 1, 1985 article, "The Reagan Doctrine proclaims overt and unashamed American support for anti-Communist revolution."

In a 1986 *New Republic* article, Krauthammer revisited the Reagan Doctrine, addressing the difficult issue of whether America's support of insurgents amounts to a support of terrorism. He proposed a three-prong test to determine whether it is moral to support insurgencies: First, there must be popular support in a rebelling colony for the insurgency. Second, the ends must be moral (e.g., establishing a democratic government would be moral while setting up a new dictatorship would not). Third and finally, the means must be moral. Krauthammer acknowledged that this last point is the most challenging test, because guerilla warfare often involves atrocities.

Krauthammer's writings on the Reagan Doctrine came to be seen as prescient in 1991 when the Soviet Union collapsed, in part, it seems, as a result of America's support for anti-Communist uprisings around the world. Years later, Krauthammer explained that he had seen that the Soviet

Union was overextended and that rebellions were resulting. Reagan, he says, "instinctively realized that one of the ways to go after the Soviets was indirect, and that is you go after their proxies, you go after their allies, you go after their clients, or even in Afghanistan you go after them directly. So that's what I called the Reagan Doctrine…"

It is important to remember, however, that the idea of a Reagan Doctrine was created by Krauthammer, and not by Reagan himself. During Reagan's second term, the President seemed to soften his vigorous anti-Soviet stance somewhat. Both he and Britain's Margaret Thatcher spoke favorably of Mikhail Gorbachev, who became the Soviet Union's general secretary in 1985. In 1983, Reagan called the Soviet Union the "Evil Empire," but by 1988 he was disavowing that label, explaining that, "I was talking about another time, another era."

Krauthammer was not the only conservative disappointed by the President's apparent retreat from the Reagan Doctrine. He was, however, outraged enough to question the President's intelligence and call his reasons for embracing Gorbachev as "ignorant and pathetic."

10. Journalistic Prestige

Krauthammer's writing began to attract attention and praise. In 1984, he received the "Champion Media Award for Economic Understanding" from Dartmouth College's Amos Tuck School of Business Administration. That same year, he received Columbia University's National Magazine Award. In 1985, he received the "First Amendment Award" from People for the American Way.

Krauthammer continued to expand his audience when he began writing a weekly column for the *Washington Post* in 1985. As he recalls, the editorial page editor Meg Greenfield approached him in 1984 to request that he write the column. He asked if he could make it a weekly column, running on Fridays (so he could have the weekend off). She agreed, and he began writing a column that would ultimately by published in four hundred newspapers each week.

1985 also saw the release of Krauthammer's first book, *Cutting Edges: Making Sense of the 80s*, a collection of his previous articles, including pieces from Time, The New Republic, and the Washington Post. Columnist George Will praised the collection, announcing that, "Already Krauthammer is a one-man saving remnant of the Democratic Party's vanishing middle." John Gross of the New York Times also praised the book, but noted that, "For all his vigilance, even Mr. Krauthammer occasionally succumbs to the columnist's occupational disease and simplifies things for the sake of a debating point."

George Will and John Gross were not the only ones identifying Krauthammer as a rising star in journalism. In 1986, Krauthammer was nominated for a Pulitzer Prize. In 1987 he succeeded at winning the Pulitzer Prize for commentary for the work he did in the *Washington Post*, joining the ranks of previous winners like William Safire and George Will. The Pulitzer Prize committee included renowned journalists from around the country, and the win was a major endorsement of his talent as a journalist. As his prestige grew, new opportunities arose.

With his growing prestige, Charles Krauthammer became comfortable writing occasional lighthearted articles and inserting some humor into his work. For example, in 1986 he wrote a Time article called "The Joy of Analog," which addressed the very real shift from analog to digital electronics, but did so in an offbeat way, with references to Star Trek and Mickey Mouse. Similarly, in 1987's "Casablanca in Color? I'm Shocked, Shocked!" he poked fun at Hollywood directors like Woody Allen who were complaining about the colorization of black-and-white films.

11. The Unipolar Moment

In international affairs, Krauthammer became interested in the fall of Communism and its aftermath. In January 1989, he wrote "The Secret of Our Success," describing the adaptability of Capitalism, and correctly predicting that Gorbachev's greatest challenge in pursuing democracy would be the "the loss of initiative, the abhorrence of risk, [and] the envy of success" among his people, which resulted from decades under Communism. In 1990, he contemplated "The German Revival," speculating that the reunification of the German nation could make Europe less unified because Germany would become very powerful relative to other European nations.

In the 1990/1991 edition of *Foreign Affairs*, Krauthammer published an article entitled, "The Unipolar Moment." He was one of the first journalists to articulate the meaning of the fall of the Soviet Union for American international politics. He realized that with the fall of the Soviet Union, the world would transition from a bipolar international political arena (i.e., the U.S. versus the Soviets) to a unipolar system in which America was the world's undisputed superpower.

Krauthammer envisioned a world in which the U.S. took the lead in international politics, with support from secondary Western powers (e.g., the U.K., Germany, Japan, and so forth). In some ways, this conceptualization proved accurate. For example, in the Gulf War of 1990 and 1991, the U.S. did, in fact, lead an international coalition of countries.

As with Krauthammer's pronouncement of the Reagan Doctrine, his articulation of the Unipolar Moment demonstrated his foresight and influence as a leading political journalist.

12. Television

In 1990, Krauthammer was invited to become a weekly panelist on PBS's roundtable program *Inside Washington*. This was the first television program to which Krauthammer was a regular contributor. The program had begun in 1988, and it was in its infancy when Krauthammer joined the panel.

Gordon Peterson hosted the program. Peterson had worked as a news personality for decades, including work as a panelist on *Agronsky & Co.*, which was the predecessor of *Inside Washington*. While he and Krauthammer formed a congenial relationship, the two frequently disagreed. In later years, Krauthammer occasionally pointed out Peterson's liberal leanings.

In the show's final episode, on December 20, 2013, Krauthammer noted to Peterson that, "[A]ll those times that I savagely attacked you for bias and twisting the news, I stand by every single one of them."

The other major panelists on the show included Nina Totenberg, Colbert King, Mark Shields, and Evan Thomas. Over time, Krauthammer came to see Totenberg, an NPR correspondent, as particularly biased in favor of the Democratic Party, and he frequently confronted her when she advocated for liberal policies.

In 1990, landing a position on a major television news panel was a significant accomplishment for Charles Krauthammer. While he would faithfully and articulately write articles for decades to come, television was the medium that would ultimately make him a household name.

13. Return to McGill

As the early 1990s progressed, Krauthammer continued to focus on the ramifications of America's new role as sole superpower. He also devoted himself to studying the development of post-Communist countries.

Personally, Krauthammer had reached a level of success as a political journalist that he could not have imagined when he graduated from college. In 1993, Krauthammer was awarded an honorary degree by his alma mater, McGill University, and he spoke at the fall commencement ceremony. It was a time for the now-prominent journalist to reflect on twenty-five years of struggle and professional growth.

He began with an apology for giving his speech in English, explaining that, "my French [has] suffered the disuse of living in a land so vast that bilingualism is considered, except for the newest of immigrants, an exotic intellectual acquirement."

He then proceeded to give the new graduates three pieces of advice. First, "don't lose your head." He mentioned Holland's tulip bulb mania, the 1636 phenomenon in which public delusion led to rampant speculation in tulip bulbs, with the bulbs increasing in price to many times a worker's annual salary, before the market crashed in early 1637. He then discussed more recent manias, like the 1980's nuclear weapon hysteria and environmental doomsday theories, reminding the students that such manias pass and that it is impossible to predict the future.

Second, he admonished them to "look outward." While acknowledging that some self-examination is necessary, he warned that, "vertiginous self-examination leads not only to a sterile moral life, but also to a stilted intellectual life."

Third, he advised them to "save the best." This was an appeal to conservatism in the broad sense, arguing that the students should not easily give up society's valuable assets. As an example, he cited the enthusiasm of some Americans to trade ethnic diversity for a focus on race.

These three pieces of wisdom provide an astute overview of Krauthammer's approach to journalism and the enduring value of his articles. Because he consciously avoids being swept up in mass hysterias, refuses to get bogged down in the subject task of self-examination, and errs on the side of preserving society's institutions, his articles tend to be timeless – still persuasive thirty years after they are written.

Take, for example, his discussion in 1983 of what he calls "plural solipsism," the belief that all people are basically the same. He wrote that, "To gloss over contradictory interests, incompatible ideologies and opposing cultures as sources of conflict is more than antipolitical. It is dangerous. Those who have long held a mirror to the world and seen only themselves are apt to be shocked and panicked when the mirror is removed, as inevitably it must be." The article refers to Russians and Iranians, but it could apply just as easily to militant Muslims and North Koreans thirty years later. The reasoning is sound and generalizable.

In his speech to the McGill graduates, Krauthammer laid out his personal intellectual philosophy. Based on twenty-five years of experience, that philosophy had proven its soundness. Now, twenty-five years later, it is equally sound.

14. Conservative Journalist

Only a few years after he began his career as a journalist, Krauthammer came to be viewed as a political conservative. The 1988 book, *Column Right: Conservative Journalists in the Service of Nationalism* by David Burner and Thomas R. West, examined four prominent conservative journalists of the time: George Will; William F. Buckley, Jr.; Irving Kristol; and Charles Krauthammer. The book did consider Krauthammer the most left-leaning of the four, acknowledging that he frequently criticized policies on both his left and his right. Despite his liberal views of certain domestic policies, however, the book cast him solidly as a conservative. Over time, he would solidify his conservative credentials further.

Throughout the 1990s, which were dominated by the Clinton presidency, Krauthammer was a voice for conservative politics. In 1993, he wrote "How Conservatism Can Come Back," arguing that "political movements need to police their extremes," concluding that, "Until it rejects the far right, conservatism will not regain the center. And without the center, it cannot win." Then, in 1996, he lamented that Presidential candidate Bob Dole failed to show the political courage necessary to win.

Krauthammer critiqued Bill Clinton more pointedly than he had critiqued prior presidents. In 1993, he accused Clinton of using the end of the Cold War as an excuse to justify his failings in Somalia, Haiti, and Bosnia. He also blasted Clinton for cozying up to President Hafez Assad of Syria and making concessions to North Korea, in an article titled

"Romancing the Thugs." These critiques seem prescient in 2017, as Syria and North Korea have become the most likely origins of global war, despite Clinton's efforts to appease them. Krauthammer repeatedly wrote of his dissatisfaction regarding Clinton's relationship with Assad. In 1998, as the country responded to the Monica Lewinsky scandal, Krauthammer asked regarding Clinton, "Is there no end to the corruption of this man?"

In the mid-1990s, Krauthammer repeatedly wrote about the importance of re-engaging in space exploration. In December 1996, he expressed his dismay that NASA had done nothing heroic in recent years – a sentiment that would be expressed by many others in the next twenty years, including private space exploration engineers and entrepreneurs like Burt Rutan and Elon Musk. Krauthammer argued that NASA should aim for a manned mission to Mars; twenty years later, President Barack Obama would announce that aim, but only after canceling the space shuttle program.

Charles Krauthammer also saw same-sex marriage as inevitable about twenty years before the rest of the country. In 1996, he wrote that, "In September the judges of the Hawaii Supreme Court are expected to legalize gay marriage. Once done there, gay marriage – like quickie Nevada divorces – will have to be recognized 'under the full faith and credit clause of the Constitution- throughout the rest of the U.S." In fact, Hawaii did not legalize same-sex marriage in 1996. Seventeen years later, in 2013, though, the state did legalize the institution. The dominos then fell just as Krauthammer predicted, with the courts (actually, the U.S. Supreme Court) ultimately legalizing same-sex marriage. In 1996, though, Krauthammer argued that it is untenable to permit gay marriage while not permitting polygamy. He would reprise his line of reasoning a decade later in an article titled "Pandora and Polygamy," which argues that legalizing same-sex marriage opens Pandora's box, leading to the legalization of polygamy.

By the end of the 1990s, Krauthammer was indisputably an established conservative. He had also begun commenting on the politics of others in the media. In a September 2000 *Washington Post* article, he noted that journalists had voted for Bill Clinton in a ratio of 13 to 1, compared to the average Americans' voting ratio of 8 to 7. He argued that this discrepancy makes liberal bias in the media unavoidable.

15. Fox News

Over the years, Krauthammer had appeared on many television news programs as a guest. By 2001, he was also regularly appearing as a guest on *Special Report* on Fox News, and other shows on Fox News had begun calling on him for political commentary, as well.

The Fox News Channel had begun broadcasting in 1996. During the ensuing four years, which featured heavy news coverage of Bill Clinton's scandals, culminating with the Lewinsky affair, conservatives increasingly turned to Fox News for coverage that avoided liberal bias. The network began attracting established conservative journalists as guests, and Krauthammer was an obvious journalist to invite.

Special Report, hosted by Brit Hume, was a Fox News mainstay from its founding. The program features a mix of news reporting and commentary. In 2007, Brit Hume left the show and was replaced by Bret Baier.

Baier notes that people frequently ask him what Charles Krauthammer is like in person. "The answer – Charles is brilliant, funny, and a very caring person. He has also been a great source of strength to me throughout all of [my son] Paul's hospitalizations."

Charles Krauthammer's appearances on Fox News would eventually lead him to develop a far broader following than he could have developed solely from print media. Because of his reserved manner, his television following has grown gradually over a period of many years.

He has also been forced to defend the conservative network from time to time. In a December 2003 article, for example, he noted that Democratic Presidential candidate Howard Dean was complaining about the political bias of Fox News, and observed that it is delusional to believe "that Americans can get their news from only one part of the political spectrum." In other words, having a conservative news outlet provides some healthy balance.

16. The Aftermath of 9/11

The terrorist attacks of September 11, 2001, brought a number of political issues to the fore – some that Krauthammer had written about for years and some that were new.

In a 1984 article titled "The New Terrorism," Krauthammer had addressed a number of issues that became important after the 9/11 attacks. He acknowledged the potential for disagreement about what constitutes "terrorism," noting "the political advantage that comes from painting the other man's freedom fighter as just another terrorist." He also noted the special threat posed by state-sponsored terrorism, which seeks to wage war instead of merely grab headlines, noting that "unlike [other types of terrorism], a single act of the new terrorism has the potential
to change history."

Krauthammer's past writings about the unipolar world were also relevant. Many countries looked to America, as the only remaining superpower, to take the lead in the fight against terrorism. Because of the unipolar dynamic, it would be difficult for the United States to define the enemy clearly.

In a December 2001 article entitled "Unilateral? Yes, Indeed," Krauthammer argued that, despite proponents of a multilateral, coalition-based approach to the war on terror, President Bush was acting unilaterally, as he should. The coalition fighting in Afghanistan, according to Krauthammer, was largely an illusion. "What exactly has Egypt contributed?"

In 2002, he addressed the question of whether Islam is inherently violent. He wrote that the question is as pointless and absurd as asking whether Christianity is inherently peaceful. Krauthammer listed a series of examples of Muslim violence against other religions, noting that, "most Muslims are obviously peaceful people living within the rules of civilized behavior. But the actual violence, bloodletting against nearly every non-Muslim civilization from Hindu to African animist, demands attention." He characterized Islam as having the "feeling of a civilization in decline."

Krauthammer was among the first to characterize America's fight against terrorism as a war. In a September 12, 2001 article, published the day after the 9/11 attacks, he wrote that, "This is not a crime. This is war." He criticized Colin Powell, the Secretary of State, for vowing to bring the perpetrators to justice. Instead, he urged that Congress issue a declaration of war. A few days later, on September 16, President George W. Bush followed Krauthammer's lead, referring to a "war on terrorism."

Not all of Krauthammer's writings about terrorism were serious, though. In the ensuing years, he occasionally took time to respond to the lunacy that resulted from America's war on terror. In a November 2010 article titled "Don't Touch My Junk," he addressed the irrationality of the TSA's airport security measures. The most absurd element, he concluded, is the screening of pilots, who would not, of, course have to be carrying a bomb in order to cause devastation on an airplane.

17. The George W. Bush Administration

Despite his credentials as a solid conservative voice and his support of the war in Afghanistan, Krauthammer refused to offer blanket support to every Republican policy. Nor did Republican politicians get a free pass from him. Although he was appointed to the President's Council on Bioethics by President George W. Bush, Krauthammer was publicly in favor of removing some restrictions on stem cell research that President Bush had authorized.

In 2002, Krauthammer was one of the Republicans who called for Senator Trent Lott's resignation after Lott made remarks that were construed as racist. At a December 5, 2002 event honoring Senator Strom Thurmond, who was retiring, Lott reportedly praised the Senator's legacy and noted that Mississippi had voted for Thurmond to be President in 1948, commenting that, "We're proud of it. And if the rest of the country had followed our lead, we wouldn't have had all these problems over all these years either." The phrase "all these problems" seems to have referred to the civil rights movement, and Krauthammer called the remarks "appalling." Lott apologized for the statement before stepping down from his position as Senate Majority Leader. The incident demonstrates Krauthammer's commitment, formed as a young man, to oppose extremists on either end of the political spectrum.

Krauthammer also opposed President Bush's foreign policy in many instances. In 2004, Krauthammer revisited his idea of unipolarity in a lecture he delivered at the American Enterprise Institute. The lecture, which centered on what he called "democratic realism," was later published by the American Enterprise Institute as a monograph titled *Democratic Realism: An American Foreign Policy for a Unipolar World,* and it would become one of Krauthammer's major contributions to US foreign policy thought. In the lecture, Krauthammer offered criticism of both the Bush Doctrine with its neoconservative traits and the so-called realism that was a part of the foreign policy of the time.

On October 4, 2005, President George W. Bush nominated Harriet Miers to replace Sandra Day O'Connor as a U.S. Supreme Court Justice. Miers had played a role in Bush's transition team when he was elected Texas governor in 1994, and Governor Bush had then appointed her chair of the Texas Lottery Commission. She had never served as a judge, however, before being nominated as a Supreme Court Justice. In her confirmation hearings, she was roundly criticized.

Krauthammer was one of the critics, noting that, "If Harriet Miers were not a crony of the president of the United States, her nomination to the Supreme Court would be a joke, as it would have occurred to no one else to nominate her." Miers withdrew from the nomination; an article Krauthammer had written a week before Miers officially withdrew from the nomination detailed a face-saving strategy that was mirrored closely by Miers' withdrawal.

18. Marcel's Passing

Although his career continued to progress, Krauthammer experienced a heavy personal loss in 2006. Krauthammer's brother, Marcel, passed away on January 17 at age 59, a victim of cancer.

Marcel had suffered from the disease for 17 years. Like Charles, he had completed medical school. Marcel, however, had continued with the profession, becoming a successful doctor. He was a pulmonologist and a professor at UCLA.

It was a heavy loss for Krauthammer, who had always been close to his brother. In a Washington Post article entitled "Marcel, My Brother," Charles Krauthammer reminisced about the way his brother had always included him in activities when he was young. Despite the four-year age gap, in childhood games the athletic Marcel insisted to his friends that "Charlie plays."

Krauthammer wrote that, "Friends and colleagues knew this part of Marcel far better than I did. We hadn't lived in the same city since he went off to medical school when I was 17. What I knew that they didn't, however, was the Marcel of before, the golden youth of our childhood together."

The loss might have turned Krauthammer's mind to the topic of mortality generally. The following year he wrote an article titled, "The Fine Art of Dying Well." The tone of the article was light, but it evidenced some deep thinking on the author's part. He discussed the fate of people whose names are appropriated for one cause or another after their deaths, as well as the dark ambition of terrorists who plot the details of their own deaths and those of others.

19. Presidential Election of 2008

Leading up to the 2008 Presidential election, Krauthammer noticed the as-yet little-known Democratic aspirant, Senator Barack Obama. He considered that, "Like many Americans, I long to see an African-American ascend to the presidency. It would be an event of profound significance, a great milestone in the unfolding story of African-Americans achieving their rightful, long-delayed place in American life."

As Obama became a serious candidate, though, Krauthammer began examining him closely, and he found certain necessary attributes lacking. In a July 27, 2007 column, he worried that Obama was a "national security amateur" trying to get elected President during a time of war.

Over the course of the 2008 Presidential election, some of Krauthammer's ideas made their way into the candidates' debates, sometimes in unexpected ways. After he wrote a piece asking the candidates to provide nuclear protection to the state of Israel, Democratic candidate Hillary Clinton parroted his ideas in her speeches.

On October 24, 2008, two weeks before the election, Krauthammer endorsed Senator John McCain, the Republican candidate. In defense of this position, he compared the foreign policy qualifications of candidates Obama and McCain. McCain clearly had a stronger resume. Despite the endorsement, though the Republican could not gather enough votes to win. Instead, Barack Obama was elected President.

After the election, in January 2009, Barack Obama attended a dinner with conservative journalists, but the dinner did little to soften Krauthammer to the President-elect. He explained that after the event, "We [journalists] sat around and said, 'Does anybody really know who he is and what he wants to do, now that we've had this?' And the answer was no. We don't know."

In the subsequent months, though, Krauthammer discovered and articulated Obama's plans. In an April 24, 2009 article entitled "Obama: The Grand Strategy," Krauthammer explained that Obama's mission was the "leveling of social inequalities," and pointed to nationalized health care, among other things, as a policy that would aid that mission.

As the Obama administration progressed, Krauthammer's evaluation proved accurate. In a January 2011 article, "The Old Obama in New Clothing," Krauthammer complained of the President's lack of fiscal responsibility, citing the government's wasteful deficit spending and the absence of any plan to reduce waste. Later, in 2012, Krauthammer explained that Obama's misguided statement about business ("If you've got a business – you didn't build that. Somebody else made that happen.") reflected the President's neglect of the virtues of national solvency and individual independence.

In 2012, he believed Republican candidate Mitt Romney would be able to beat the incumbent Obama. That hope, however, was not realized. Krauthammer noted that, "Romney is a good man who made the best argument he could, and nearly won."

20. Bestselling Author

During the Obama administration, Krauthammer continued to address hot-button issues. For example, in 2008 he published an article called "The Church of Global Warming," in which he characterized himself as a "global warming agnostic" – someone who believes that carbon dioxide pollution cannot be good, but that global warming advocates are not reliable.

After three decades in journalism, Krauthammer had developed a large library of opinion pieces, but it had been decades since he had published a book.

In 2013, Krauthammer released a full-length book, *Things That Matter: Three Decades of Passions, Pastimes and Politics*. The material contained within *Things That Matter* was compiled from selected works that Krauthammer had written throughout his career. The essays included discussions on America's role in the world, bioethics (Krauthammer had been appointed in 2002 to President Bush's President's Council on Bioethics), and the future of Israel and Jewish people. The book's introduction included an autobiography that was written specifically for the book.

In the book, Krauthammer provides some insight into why he has chosen to spend a career writing about politics: "Politics, the crooked timber of our communal lives, dominates everything… You can have the most advanced and efflorescent of cultures. Get your politics wrong, however, and everything stands to be swept away." There is ample evidence to support this conclusion. For example, in a 2013 report, The Economist argued persuasively that the four

Nordic countries (i.e., Sweden, Denmark, Finland, and Norway) are both the highest overall economic performers and the best-governed countries. At any rate, Krauthammer's work has shown his commitment to improving government.

In its first year, *Things That Matter* sold over a million copies, and it continues to sell. It was the number one New York Times bestseller for ten weeks. Reflecting on the book's surprising success, Krauthammer said that, "I wrote *Things That Matter* to leave something behind of my ideas and my prose in case I got hit by a bus. Instead, I seem to have won the lottery. How gratifying to find that the book has appealed to so wide and enthusiastic a readership."

Krauthammer's years of extensive writing and political punditry have earned him a position as one of the most respected conservative commentators; even some liberals are quick to offer praise of him. In an article by Politico's Ben Smith, Krauthammer has been described as one of the central figures in opposition to President Obama. Krauthammer was described as "the most important conservative columnist" by the New York Times' David Brooks. His vocal support of intervention in both Afghanistan and Iraq after 9/11 endeared him to many conservative-minded individuals.

In addition to the Pulitzer award, Krauthammer has, at various times, received accolades and recognitions for his work and influence. In 2006, the Financial Times named him the most influential commentator in the United States. Two years earlier, the American Enterprise Institute gave him the Irving Kristol Award. Krauthammer was also awarded the Eric Breindel Award for Excellence in Opinion Journalism as well as the first Bradley Prize. In 2013, he was given the

William F. Buckley Award for Media Excellence. Krauthammer is a member of the Council on Foreign Relations.

21. Presidential Election of 2016

The 2016 Presidential election was challenging for Charles Krauthammer. In his view, the large field of Republican candidates included several excellent options. The frontrunner and ultimately winner, however, was a man Krauthammer would never have chosen: Donald Trump. As a candidate, Trump was the antithesis of Krauthammer – boisterous, spontaneous, and crass. Trump also failed to follow Krauthammer's advice that Republicans should denounce the extremists in their party, instead welcoming fringe elements that Democratic candidate Hillary Clinton called "deplorables."

In a June 4, 2015 appearance on Special Report with Bret Baier, Krauthammer reviewed statistics regarding which candidates Republicans said they would never vote for, in a recent poll. Donald Trump led the list. Krauthammer explained that, "[Trump] is going to say how sad it is that I'm saying these things, but, you know, this is an open forum and we have free speech. He has a well-deserved and, I would say, an impressive 59 percent."

As predicted, Trump did not appreciate Krauthammer's comment. That night, he sent out three separate tweets about Krauthammer:

One of the worst and most boring political pundits on television is @krauthammer. A totally overrated clown who speaks without knowing facts

.@krauthammer pretends to be a smart guy, but if you look at his record, he isn't. A dummy who is on too many Fox shows. An overrated clown!

Dummy political pundit @krauthammer constantly pressed the crazy war in Iraq. Many lives and trillions of dollars wasted. U.S. got NOTHING!

"@krauthammer: On sale today. Things That Matter in paperback. With a new section on the Obama years. Book sucks!

Of all Trump's campaign antics, his repeated accusations about foreigners seemed to bother Krauthammer most. In a July 2015 appearance on *Special Report with Bret Baier*, Krauthammer called Trump a "rodeo clown" and ridiculed his failure to "make a distinction between legal and illegal immigrants when he said that an entire immigrant group [i.e., Mexican immigrants] are rapists."

Despite his misgivings about Trump, though, Krauthammer could not stomach the "bottomless cynicism" of Hillary Clinton. Three weeks before the November 8, 2016 election, he lamented that, "I will not vote for Hillary Clinton. But, as I've explained in these columns, I could never vote for Donald Trump."

The week before the election, Krauthammer believed the odds favored a Clinton win. Like many in the media, though, he was surprised when Trump won handily.

Although Donald Trump was not Krauthammer's preferred candidate, the conservative journalist immediately knew what

Trump's election meant for America. Speaking on The Kelly File on November 11, 2016, Krauthammer concluded that: "Obama's legacy is toast.... He knew that so much of his accomplishments had been built on ramming stuff through the House and the Senate with very little consensus, in fact none on ObamaCare coming from the Republicans, on executive orders that are reversible with the stroke of a pen, on regulation that is easily reversible, that it collapses if and when his successor turns out to be a Republican."

Krauthammer was also a good sport about Trump's win, noting that "What Donald Trump did was historic... and he deserves all the credit for it." He observed that Trump won by appealing to white, working-class people who were ignored by the other candidates, but who were largely responsible for Ronald Reagan's victory thirty-six years earlier.

22. Conclusions

As the Trump Presidency continues, Charles Krauthammer will doubtless have many insights to provide his readers and viewers. Like most Americans, he clearly hopes for the best in the years to come. As he proved during the George W. Bush administration, though, he will not cut a president any slack, even if that president is a Republican.

While Krauthammer is widely known for his political journalism, that is, of course, not his only pursuit. In his private life, Krauthammer is a successful husband father. Charles and Robyn have a son, Daniel, who received a degree in economics from Harvard and then traveled to Oxford to complete a graduate degree in economics before studying at Standford's business school.

He has also pursued philanthropic activities of interest. Together with his wife Robyn, Krauthammer founded Pro Musica Hebraica in 2004. The not-for-profit organization aims to bring classical Jewish music to wider audiences in concert settings. Although he is not religious, Krauthammer identifies strongly with Jewish culture, and is working to preserve the music of that culture.

Krauthammer's work as a journalist has familial and philanthropic elements, too. While his father's life is the story of 20th-century immigration, his own life has been dedicated to making America a place to which immigrants would wish to come. He has steadfastly advocated for a rational government that protects civil liberties and stands up to bullies around the world.

Over a long career in journalism Charles Krauthammer has also inspired widespread support. Perhaps part of the reason Krauthammer has garnered respect from liberals, despite his strong conservative stance on foreign policy, is because of the progressive stance he has taken on certain issues.

Despite his willingness to take a stand on hard issues, Krauthammer has continued to be well-liked by the vast majority of his associates, and even by his political opponents. His astute views continue to enlighten America's political discourse, while his culture and personal virtues enlighten its character.

Made in the USA
Lexington, KY
23 June 2018